B Geh
Greenberg, Jan, 1
Frank O. Gehry

W9-BLZ-827

STONY CREEK LIBRARY
1350 GREENFIELD PIKE
NOBLESVILLE, IN 46060

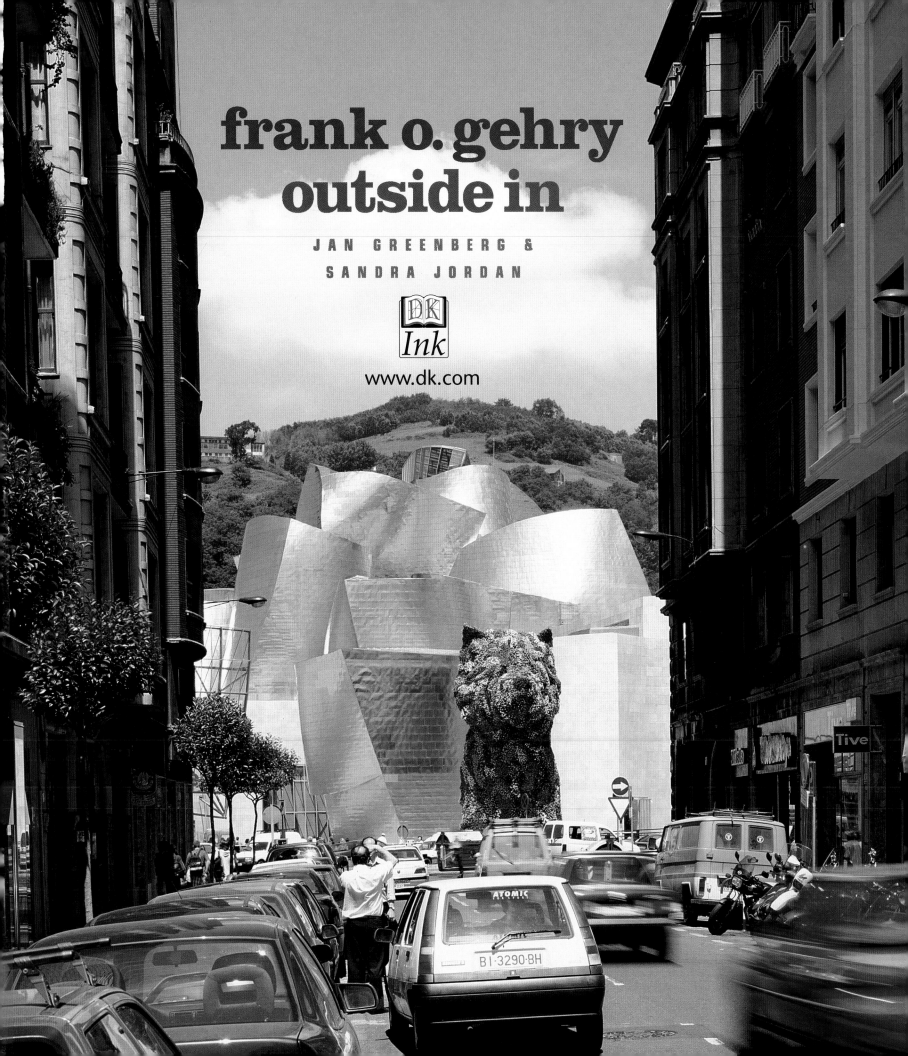

frank o. gehry
outside in

JAN GREENBERG &
SANDRA JORDAN

Ink

www.dk.com

For George Nicholson

www.dk.com

Dorling Kindersley Publishing, Inc.
95 Madison Avenue
New York, New York 10016

Text copyright © 2000 by Jan Greenberg and Sandra Jordan
"Fred & Ginger in Prague: The Frank Gehry Building"
copyright © 2000 by Bobbi Katz
CATIA is a registered trademark of Dassault Systemes, Suresnes, France.

Endpaper photographs taken at Frank O. Gehry's office.

All rights reserved. No part of this publication may be reproduced or
transmitted in any form or by any means, electronic, photocopying, recording,
or otherwise, without the prior written permission of the publisher.

Dorling Kindersley books are available at special discounts for bulk
purchases for sales promotions or premiums. Special editions, including
personalized covers, excerpts of existing guides, and corporate imprints
can be created in large quantities for specific needs. For more information,
contact Special Markets Dept., Dorling Kindersley Publishing, Inc.,
95 Madison Ave., New York, NY 10016; fax: (800) 600-9098.

Library of Congress Cataloging-in-Publication Data
Greenberg, Jan [date]
Frank O. Gehry: Outside In / Jan Greenberg and Sandra Jordan.—1st ed.
p.   cm.
Includes bibliographical references and index.
ISBN 0-7894-2677-3
1. Gehry, Frank O., 1929– —Criticism and interpretation. 2. Architecture,
Postmodern—United States.
I. Jordan, Sandra (Sandra Jane Fairfax). II. Title.
NA737.G44 G74 2000
720'.92—dc21   99-046871

Book design by Dirk Kaufman.
The text of this book is set in 16 point Fournier.
Printed and bound in the United States.

First Edition, 2000
2 4 6 8 10 9 7 5 3 1

contents

Boat Gallery, Guggenheim Museum, Bilbao, Spain

THINK.

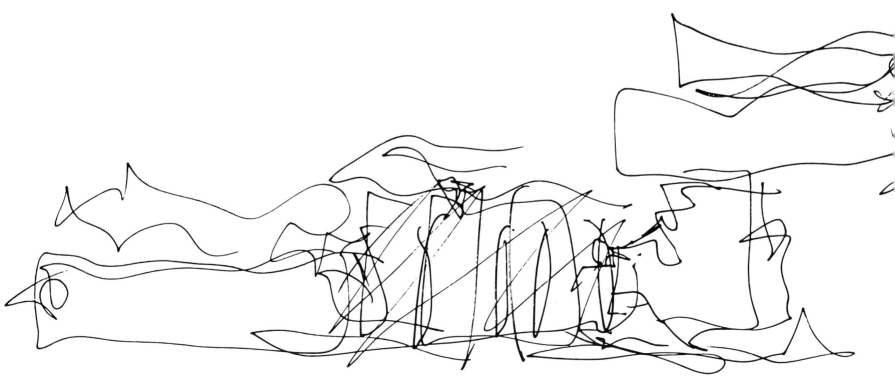

DIFFERENT

When Frank Gehry was ten years old, his family went on vacation to a lake near their home in Canada. "We stayed in a cabin. There was a lady there who read handwriting. She read mine and told my mother that someday this guy is going to be a famous architect. I heard her say it, but I didn't pay much attention. I wasn't sure what an architect did. And besides, when you're a kid, you don't believe anything good is going to happen."

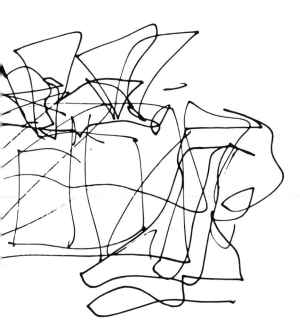

These days it's hard to pin Frank O. Gehry down. But when he's not off giving lectures or checking on projects, you usually can find him in Los Angeles at the rambling warehouse space he calls his studio. From his modest glass cubicle, he looks out at an office bustling with young architects working on more than thirty Frank Gehry buildings in progress. What makes Gehry's designs stand out is his gift for changing the ordinary into the amazing. His buildings surge with energy and movement, revealing forms never before seen in architecture.

Frank O. Gehry's sketches for the Guggenheim Museum, Bilbao, Spain

Short and slightly rumpled, with a shock of white hair and an amused expression, the California guru of modern architecture comes off more maverick than elder statesman. People recognize him on the streets and in restaurants. A banner with Gehry's photograph, advertising Apple computers, hangs on the exterior of a building. THINK DIFFERENT, it commands. There are similar banners of Albert Einstein and John Lennon. Heady company for a man whose neighbors once picketed the house he built for himself. Gehry is used to being called controversial. Now critics are hailing him as "a genius." "I'm being geniused to death," he says.

This barrage of publicity results from a startling building, the Guggenheim Museum in Bilbao, Spain. Since it opened in 1997, it's been on magazine covers and in newspapers around the world. Suddenly Gehry finds himself the center of international acclaim. But he can still remember years of struggling to pay his bills while turning his back on jobs that didn't interest him.

The Guggenheim Museum in Bilbao

I'M BEING GENIUSED TO DEATH

"Buildings can have an important role. Churchill said we make our buildings and our buildings make us. There is something to that."

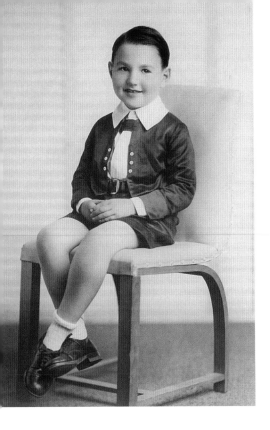

(above) Frank as a child

(left) Walker Museum, Minneapolis. *This sparkling fish sculpture rises twenty-two feet in the air. Its glass scales were assembled piece by piece.*

(below) Etchings of carp

As a boy the closest he came to architecture was concocting cities out of blocks and scraps of wood his grandmother brought home from the fix-it shop around the corner. "She would go and get these cuttings. There would be a piece of plywood with a hole in the middle, or a broken corner, or a long, funny piece. She'd sit on the floor with me, and we'd make cities." When he was eighteen and trying to decide what to do with his life, the memory of his grandmother and those wooden cities kept coming back to him. "Here was an adult saying you could be grown up and still play. That's real creativity."

Gehry's grandmother was his best friend. He says she believed in strange, magical powers and superstitions. "When somebody would look at me funny, she would lick my face! I hated that, but I loved her a lot."

Young Frank often spent the night at his grandparents' house. They had emigrated to Canada from Poland, and although they slowly adopted the ways of their new country, they observed their Jewish traditions. On Thursdays, Frank went to the market with his grandmother. Each week she bought a live carp to be made into gefilte fish for Sabbath supper. They carried it home in a heavy white paper bag filled with water.

"We'd put it in the bathtub, and I would watch this fish for a day, this beautiful object swimming around. Then the next day it would be gone," he says. Those beautiful disappearing fish, still vivid in his memories, appear over and over in Gehry's architecture.

As a teenager he worked off and on in his grandparents' hardware store. There, surrounded by nuts and bolts, pipes and chains, glass and wood, Frank became fascinated with everyday materials. His grandfather, a scholar of the Talmud, the book of Jewish law, came from a family of union organizers in Poland. He and Frank took long walks, discussing politics and religion.

Frank was just entering junior high when his father moved the family to Timmins, a gold-mining town in Ontario, to open a vending and slot machine business. It was a small town compared with Toronto, but his father's business prospered, and the family settled into the community.

"I was an average student with moments of brilliance like any kid. Mostly I was a loner, shy and quiet. I spent a lot of time reading *Popular Mechanics.*" Even though he was small, he was athletic. His father had been a boxer, and Frank liked the rough-and-tumble of sports. "Since I couldn't play football, I was a cheerleader."

In Timmins, Frank ran into his first experience with anti-Semitism. A group of bullies tormented him at school, beating him up and calling him Fish, an insult suggesting that he smelled. It was humiliating to be punched and taunted because he was Jewish. During this painful time he pulled back from his family's religious beliefs. He even wrote an

How to Look at a Building

Most buildings are easy to describe. They usually are squares or rectangles with pitched or flat roofs. Bilbao is totally different. But no matter what the shape or size, you can look at all buildings using the same questions.

A Few Questions & Some Answers

Q: Stand back. Look up. It's big. It's wild!
What's it for?

A: This is the Guggenheim Museum in
Bilbao, Spain. It exhibits contemporary
art from all over the world.

Q: What is the site? What is around it?

A: The banks of a river, surrounded by
older, more traditional buildings in the
heart of a big city.

Q: What materials is the building made of?

A: Titanium, glass, steel, and limestone.

*How do you look at the museum in terms of its
design elements—color, line, texture, and form?*

Q: What is the color?

A: The colors are silver, gold, gray, and blue
from the reflection of the sky and sun.

Q: What are the lines of the building?

A: The lines are curvy; hardly a straight
line exists.

Q: What is the texture?

A: It looks slick, shiny, and hard, but the
titanium is springy to the touch.

Q: What is the form?

A: The odd geometric forms are all different
and seem to pile up and out from the
central core. The form of the outside or
exterior defines the space in the interior.
The shapes change as you walk around it.

Q: What are some words that describe the
building? Use your five senses to find
qualities that are vivid in terms of sight,
sound, touch, taste, and smell.

A: Everyone has their own list. What's yours?

Q: What is the feeling expressed by the
museum in Bilbao? What does it remind
you of? It is inviting or menacing?
Energetic or peaceful?

A: To us it looks like a giant sculpture.
We are reminded of a spaceship, an
iceberg, or the sails of a ship.

essay with a classmate at school defending atheism. For years after that he ignored his ethnic identity, but it simmered just below the surface.

Many artists use autobiographical images to work through their conflicts. For Gehry, the shape of a fish repeated over and over in his designs represents his mixed feelings. On one hand, the fish echoes the anti-Semitic slurs of his childhood. On the other, it symbolizes the comforting religious rituals observed by his grandmother. The giant fish sculptures elevate memory into art.

Anti-Semitism wasn't his only source of trouble. His father's business in Timmins collapsed when Canada passed laws making slot machines illegal. The family moved back to Toronto and opened a small store, but it quickly went bankrupt. Frank's father fell apart under the pressure. It was Frank who helped his mother auction off their belongings and move to Los Angeles, with its booming economy and relatives to help them start over.

"We were middle class in Canada, but by the time we got to L.A. we were very, very poor. We were down at the bottom," says Gehry. He lived with his parents and sister in a small apartment, drove a truck, and installed breakfast nooks to pay for school at night. He says, "I worked hard, but I enjoyed it. It was manly, macho, to be a kid driving a truck."

As Gehry drove around Los Angeles, he noticed the flat light so different from that of the Canadian landscape. The city was growing, and every day he saw new buildings popping up haphazardly, most of them badly made.

This huge flying fish made of bronze-colored stainless steel floats above the pool of a hotel in Barcelona, Spain.

He was taking art classes at the University of Southern California, but he decided to switch his major to architecture.

I STILL CRY WHENEVER I GO INSIDE THIS CHAPEL

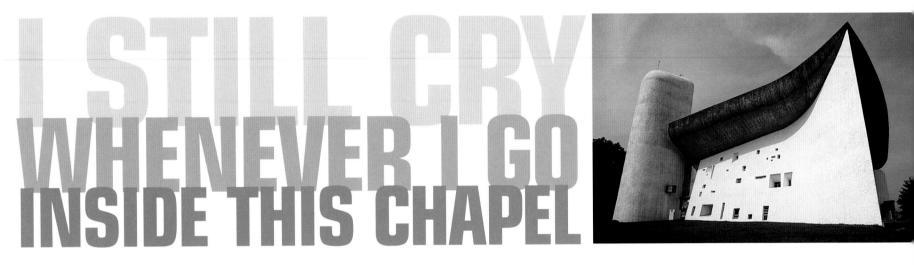

Notre-Dame-du-Haut (1955), Ronchamp, France, designed by Le Corbusier

While he was in school, he married, and after graduation he and his wife, Anita, moved to Cambridge, Massachusetts, so he could study urban planning at Harvard. But endless discussions of theory and classes in statistics bored him. He dropped out. For the rest of the year he audited only those classes at the university that sparked his imagination, such as art, music, philosophy, and politics.

One of his classmates was putting together a small exhibit of paintings by the French architect Le Corbusier. When Gehry saw the show, it struck him that the forms of Le Corbusier's architecture came from the organic shapes in his paintings. It was possible, he realized, to break away from the square box of most buildings. "That's when I threw the grid away, and said, 'Man, there's another freedom out there, and that's the place I want to be.' "

getting into

Entrance to the Gehry house in
Santa Monica, California

o the game

How does an architect get started? For Gehry it was a no-frills beginning. "I got one client; that was all I needed. I had twenty dollars in my pocket, a wife, and two daughters. We were struggling, and this guy called me and said he was going to give me a job. Two thousand bucks he paid me. It was a small warehouse building, the company headquarters, and I added a facade and a garden."

Gehry had worked for several architecture firms before striking out on his own, and his former employers sent him some remodeling jobs. Slowly the clients came. "I think it's word of mouth. Somebody would tell somebody that they knew somebody who was good or something. And they called me."

As he searched for his own style, he realized he had more in common with the methods of cutting-edge West Coast artists than with the standard fare of other architects. "The artists were working with inexpensive materials—broken wood and paper— and they were making beauty." They in turn were aware of Gehry's work, and when he visited his building sites, he'd often find them poking around. "After a while we became friends, like being part of a big family."

Gehry designed studios for several of them, constructed of galvanized metal, shingles, and unpainted plywood—funky unfinished textures typical of his early style. The artists' studios caused a lot of talk, but it was his own house that shot him into the architectural spotlight.

What's New?
or How Frank Gehry's House Is (Probably) Different from Yours
...and Why

- You can see the pink walls of the old house wrapped inside the new house.
- *"I didn't want to destroy it. I thought if I built a house around it so you could look inside and see the old house, there would be some historical continuity for the neighborhood."*

- He uses funky, unorthodox building materials: tin for walls, asphalt for kitchen floors, chain-link fences, unpainted plywood.
- *"They're cheap, but they look great. We use these materials for anonymous industrial buildings. Using them in housing and upscale construction gives us a new take on them."*

- Many of the ceiling beams and joists are exposed and raw.
- *"Buildings look most interesting before they are finished."*

- Some of the pipes and plumbing are uncovered.
- *"If things look good when they are installed, why cover them up?"*

- The house has things in common with a piece of modern sculpture. It looks different from every angle.
- *"Life is chaotic, dangerous, and surprising. Buildings should reflect it."*

- The house is playful and doesn't take itself too seriously.
- *To Gehry, houses should be fun. And at heart he's a big kid with the best set of Legos in the world.*

Frank and Anita Gehry had divorced, and a few years later he had married Berta, an energetic young woman from Panama (who now manages his office). With a young son and hopes for another child, they had outgrown a crowded apartment. Since Gehry couldn't afford to build their dream house, Berta and his mother went house shopping. They found a two-story pink bungalow on a quiet street in Santa Monica, a suburb of Los Angeles. He couldn't imagine living in such a conventional house, so with very little money, he set about remodeling. Since he was his own client, he felt free to experiment. Is a wall still a wall if it's made of chain link? How can a building give a feeling of movement and energy? Why should the skeleton of a house, the beams and joists that hold it up, be covered by drywall or paneling?

His answers to these questions, reflected in his remodeling of the tidy, shingled cottage, left his neighbors outraged. They signed petitions and demanded the city council take action. Gehry says he was caught off guard by their reactions. Many of his neighbors had campers or boats parked in their driveways. To him there wasn't that much difference between the texture of metal walls on a house and metal walls on a camper or boat. He says, "It was the same aesthetic, but they couldn't see it."

LIFE IS CHAOTIC

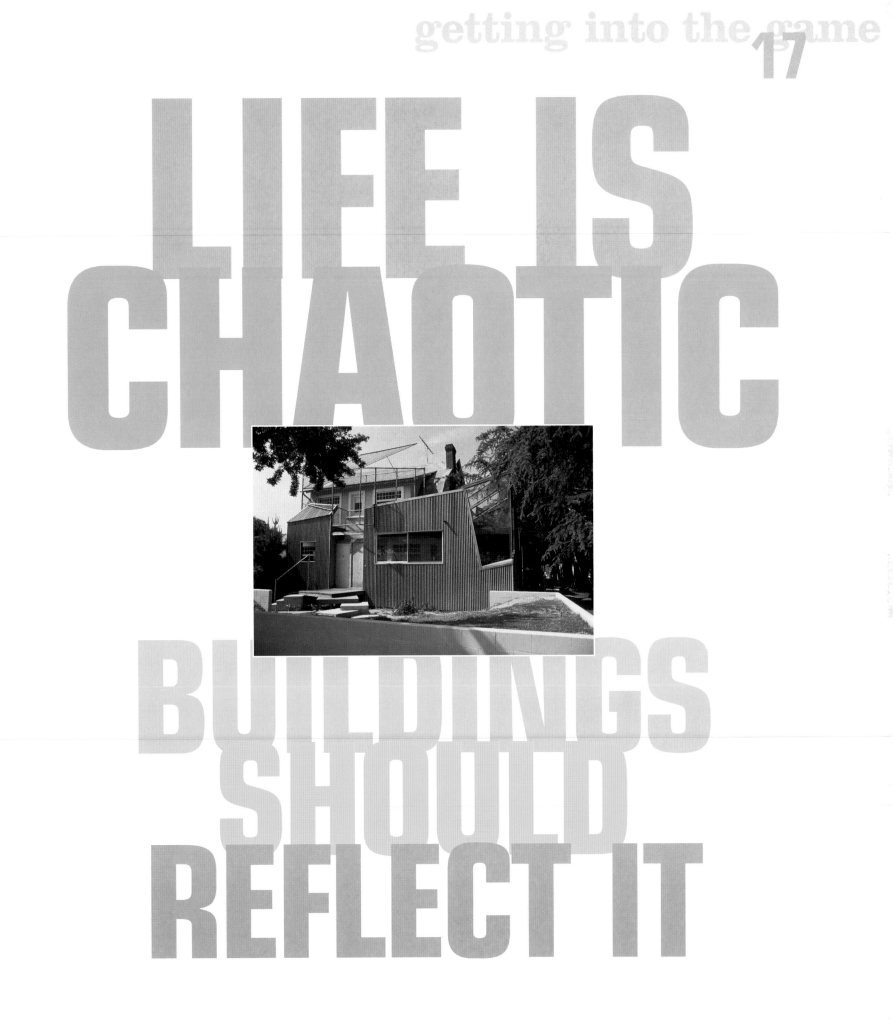

BUILDINGS SHOULD REFLECT IT

Twenty years are a lifetime in Los Angeles, a city that changes almost overnight. The neighborhood has become fancier, but the Gehry house fits in somehow. What seemed shocking twenty years ago makes us curious today. The house is still one of a kind, but our eye has become used to the new forms and unlikely materials. Part of the job of artists and architects is to show us what we will like next year or in ten years, not what we already like.

These days, instead of hostile neighbors, sidewalk visitors are fans of architecture who have come to see for themselves the house that acted as a laboratory for Frank Gehry's work. "We can be sitting down to a late dinner when out of the darkness come flashes of light," says Berta. "We take a look, and there is a busload of tourists on the sidewalk taking souvenir photographs."

"Whenever the buses came, my brother, Sam, and I would dress up as soldiers and march back and forth, pretending we were guards—to stop people from peering in windows," says Gehry's older son, Alejandro, now grown up and a graphic designer and illustrator. "The house was great for kids. Our friends loved to come over and act out *Star Wars* on the different levels."

Interior views of the Gehry house

I WORK
I JUST J
LEARN T(

The house changed Gehry's life in more ways than one. In 1978 Gehry's biggest client was in town for the opening of a forty-million-dollar shopping center that Gehry had designed. The man came to dinner at the Gehrys' house soon after the first set of renovations were finished. With gusto Frank tells the story of what happened next.

"So this client said, 'I don't understand your house. Do you really like it?' and I said, 'Yeah!'

"So he said, 'If you really like this house, then you don't like that,' and he pointed to the blueprints for the shopping center we had just finished. I said, 'It's not as good.'

"Then he said, 'Well, why don't you stop building shopping centers?' And I said, 'Because there aren't any clients for my house,' and he said, 'You'll find them.' So we shook hands and agreed that we wouldn't work together." Frank laughs. "That was scary, but I felt good about it. When the conversation took place, I had forty people working for my firm. Within a month I was down to three."

After that evening Gehry started refusing projects that required him to compromise. The chances he took might be called foolhardy by outsiders, but to Gehry they were merely getting on with his real work.

INTUITIVELY.
UMP IN AND
SWIM LATER.

cardboar

As this picture proves, the Easy Edges chairs were stronger than they looked at first glance.

d cutups

Frank Gehry says, "You can turn junk into a virtue." He always liked the idea of taking cheap materials and using them. What others labeled "a throwaway," Gehry not only recycled but transformed. Like Rumpelstiltskin, who turned straw into gold, he turned a stack of cardboard into a chair. The wiggly chair became the model for a new line of furniture called Easy Edges. It's not unusual for architects to design furniture to go with their buildings, but not of cardboard. Where did he come up with this concept?

One day, Gehry recounts, he was staring at the edge of one of his project models in his office. The profile view took on a new shape in his mind's eye. "I started thinking. Here was this corrugated cardboard, and I could make it into a chair, cut one out in a hour. I'd sketch it in the morning, and the guys in the studio could build them. By afternoon I'd have three or four to test."

To manufacture a cardboard chair in 1972 cost seven dollars; it sold for thirty-five dollars, a product that anyone could afford. It fit Gehry's strong views about being socially responsible in his work. He and an artist friend drew up seventeen cardboard pieces—from chairs to dining room tables to rockers—for the Easy Edges line. They were sturdy, practical, and cheap.

Making furniture, Frank says, was "like fast food, quick nourishment. It moves; it's built; it's done."

Department stores were excited about Easy Edges, and sales took off, but Frank says, "The publicity overwhelmed me. Overnight every newspaper in the country had pictures." What had started out as revolutionary had become fashionable. The side of Gehry that was a nonconformist, a rebel, shied away from this kind of success.

After three months, in spite of brisk sales, he canceled the project. Mass-producing the chairs would take all his time. He was determined to make his contribution as an architect, not as a designer. Once again Gehry walked away from a successful commercial venture that stood in the way of his goals.

Five years later he developed a line of large, shaggy armchairs called Experimental Edges, which was produced in smaller quantities and shown mostly in galleries.

Frank on the ice with a bentwood chair
He says his favorite possession is a hockey stick personally signed by Wayne Gretzky, aka the Great One.

Most recently he came out with an elegant line of blond bentwood chairs inspired by bushel baskets he played with as a child in Toronto. Gehry also tried his hand at making lamps. In 1983 he entered a competition held by the Formica Corporation to create a lamp out of a new translucent plastic called Colorcore.

One day, frustrated by his awkward attempts, he smashed the lamp on the floor. It splintered into pieces with jagged edges that reminded him of fish scales or sharks' teeth. From the shards a whimsical fish lamp was hatched.

The fish imagery refers back to his childhood, but Gehry says that the fish also appeals to him as a primitive symbol, like the snake. It darts in and out of his imagination, scribbled on his sketches, "whenever I'd draw something and I couldn't finish the design."

(Top) Experimental Edges armchair

(Second from top) Colorcore fish lamp
First the fish was carved out of wood. A wire armature was stretched over it. The wire was cut and resoldered after the wood was removed. The fish, with a light bulb placed inside, rests on a base of shards.

(Second from bottom) Colorcore fish lamp

(Bottom) Snake lamp

(Right) Sketch of bentwood armchair

STONY CREEK LIBRARY
1350 GREENFIELD PIKE
NOBLESVILLE, IN 46060

A view of the Loyola University Law School campus in Los Angeles, California

(Inset left) Aerial view of Loyola

(Inset right) The Roman Forum in Rome, Italy

G HAS A STORY

Frank Gehry designs and oversees the construction of spaces and places where people live, work, and play. People who seek him out expect the unexpected. He says, "My approach is different. There are no rules, no right or wrong. I work intuitively. I just jump in and learn to swim later."

A young architect who works with him says, "Frank always spends time with clients finding out what they want. Sometimes they won't really know, and he has to push them. 'How are you going to use the building? What do you need to make it work for you?' That's a very important part of the process." Architects refer to this as the program.

Gehry also must consider the budget, or how much money the client is willing to spend. When the Loyola University Law School called on him back in 1978, the school consisted of one building and a parking garage in a run-down area of Los Angeles. With big dreams and a tight budget, the administration called for a program that could be done in stages as it raised the money. Number one on its wish list was a sense of community for the campus. The faculty and students had their own lists.

"They asked if the new building could say something about the law," says Frank. "Just coincidentally, at about that time I went to Rome and I visited the Roman Forum. I thought: This is the beginning of the law and the courts."

What he saw there—broken columns, fragments, individual structures scattered around a square—he incorporated into his master plan for Loyola. Nothing very tall. No repetitions. A variety of sizes, shapes, colors, and materials. The result feels as if a small town, or what Gehry calls a village of forms, had grown up over many years.

In contrast to Loyola's drab urban setting, the site of the Schnabel residence is a quiet, private street in Los Angeles, surrounded by grass and trees. Yet Gehry applied some of the same architectural solutions. Once again he created a village of forms, though on a smaller scale.

Mrs. Schnabel grew up visiting the Griffith Observatory near her home in L.A. She told Frank, "When I was a little girl, I always wanted to live in the observatory and look at the stars." Gehry says, "I try to realize my clients' fantasies and create something special for them." For the Schnabel house he included a fanciful copper dome, an echo of Griffith Park.

"The design process works both ways," says an associate. "That's why Frank wants a client with an opinion, someone who's going to play the game with him and push him to the next level."

The Schnabel residence, Los Angeles

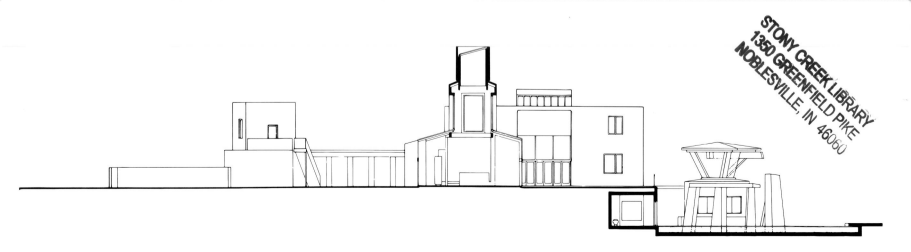

Back view of the Schnabel house
*When you look at a piece of modern sculpture, you can't always predict from
the front what the back will look like. The view changes as you walk around it.
Gehry designs houses are like that, too.*

(Below) Architectural drawing of a side elevation of the Schnabel house

STONY CREEK LIBRARY
1350 GREENFIELD PIKE
NOBLESVILLE, IN 46060

the client went for it

Chiat/Day is an advertising agency known for its inventive Nike and Apple computer ads. It needed an office on a small site in Venice, a beach town near L.A. The final plan called for seventy-five thousand square feet of offices on three floors in three separate sections. Gehry thought of a curved boatlike shape for one structure and tree forms for the other. But he was struggling with the third element.

One day Gehry and his client Jay Chiat were looking critically at the model. Chiat kept pushing Gehry for more. On a nearby table sat a small replica of the red binoculars the sculptors Claes Oldenburg and Coosje van Bruggen had proposed as a form for a library in Italy. Gehry picked up the binoculars, then plunked them down on the model. "Why not build the middle building like this?" he asked.

(Above) Binoculars Building in Venice, California
The binoculars are not mere decoration. They house a meeting room on the second floor.

(Left) Sketch by Claes Oldenburg and Coosje van Bruggen for proposed building in Italy

"The client went for it," says Frank. He brought Oldenburg and van Bruggen to L.A. as collaborating artists on the building. Gehry admits he looks for awkward connections, like a "jazz player slightly off key." In this building the binoculars went from an awkward connection to a daring conclusion.

On a clear day, gleaming in the sunlight, the Binoculars Building brings a smile: an L.A. landmark amid the jumble of cars, minimalls, and endless freeways. On a smoggy day the black binoculars loom like Darth Vader about to stalk his enemies. It is roadside architecture, meant to be seen from a car as people travel down Main Street.

The binoculars remind us of twin towers. In turn twin towers remind us of another Gehry office building, the Nationale-Nederlanden, in the historic section of Prague, in the Czech Republic. During World War II an American plane accidentally dropped a bomb there. For Gehry, who is sensitive to the history of a site, this dramatic story made a deep impression. But the biggest problem he had to solve involved neighbors who insisted their view of Prague Castle be left open. Before anything could be built, the public had to vote on the plans. "They saw every drawing, every model," says Frank. "I was sorry when something didn't work, but I wanted them to see the struggle."

The Nationale-Nederlanden in Prague, Czech Republic

For most projects his design process seems leisurely. After a number of quick sketches Gehry makes the first of many models. Again and again he revises. "I'll move a wall on a model, look at it for two weeks, then move it again. And I worry about things. I'm like a mother hen." He once called the process "weird, like watching paint dry it is so slow." But he also admits, "I don't really think it's weird. I work hard. The design changes over time, and I struggle with it. I'm trying to solve problems."

At last there was a final model. "We got sixty-eight percent of the vote," says Gehry. "The president was for it, and his wife was against it."

The finished building has two towers, one glass, the other precast concrete with a plaster finish. Halfway up, the glass building tapers in to allow the neighbors their view of the castle. It brings to mind a female figure with a curvy body. The public nicknamed the building Fred and Ginger after the American movie stars Fred Astaire and Ginger Rogers, as if one tower were a dancer being spun by the other. There's a feeling of gaiety in this description of the dancing building, though it also retains the darker history of the site. The glass tower with its hour-glass shape and leaning pillars might be imploding from a bomb, about to collapse in on itself.

Four different projects, four different, equally satisfying solutions. But Gehry was about to face the biggest challenge of his career: a building whose mission was to save a city.

(Right) Fred Astaire and Ginger Rogers step out in *Swing Time*

(Opposite) The Nationale-Nederlanden (Fred and Ginger), Prague

THE FRANK GEHRY BUILDING: FRED & GINGER IN PRAGUE

Such
magic
happens
when they meet
that
each
alone
seems
incomplete.
With
elegance
they
dance
they
glide
gracing movie screens worldwide.
Watch   the   way
that   they
relate
even   as
they   separate.

"Fred & Ginger"
began to mean
a perfect couple
in *any* scene.
Now
ALL Prague wonders
if
(perchance)
glass and plaster
just might . . .
dance!

BOBBI KATZ

the silver dre

Frank Gehry in front of the
Guggenheim Museum, Bilbao, Spain
*"When I was a student, I used to hear
that Frank Lloyd Wright could visualize
the whole building, inside and out, when
it was still in the planning stage, and I
thought, What a wonderful thing.
But now I can do it. Practice helps."*

eam machine

The story of Bilbao reads like a fairy tale. The proud port city in the Basque region of northern Spain had survived fires, floods, and civil war in its seven hundred years. But by 1990 the once-handsome city had fallen on hard times. Shipyards sat idle; steel mills, silent.

Faced with widespread unemployment and irate citizens, the city fathers and government officials put their heads together and came up with a bold scheme. Their master plan included a first-class museum, so original that it would attract worldwide attention and rescue their town from its slow decline. But they couldn't do it alone.

Guggenheim Museum (1956) in New York City, designed by American architect Frank Lloyd Wright

They called on Thomas Krens, the powerful head of the Guggenheim Museum, headquartered in New York City. A new Guggenheim in Spain appealed to Krens. To continue the museum's tradition of great architecture, he announced a competition.

Three architects from Austria, Japan, and the United States were invited to submit proposals. In 1991 Frank Gehry and his wife, Berta, who speaks fluent Spanish, went to Bilbao. Enthusiastic about the city but not the site, Gehry and Krens offered a suggestion. Instead of redoing a warehouse in the town's old historic district, what about a new site across town on a bend in the Nervión River? The tall bridge spanning the river would cross through the museum and become an integral part of the composition.

True to form, Gehry submitted a radical design, a model he constructed of sheets of paper rolled and taped by hand, like a sculptor molding clay. Everyone knew his plan went beyond all expectations. The big question was, Could it be built?

The secret weapon was a three-dimensional imaging computer program developed by the French aerospace industry to design fighter planes, CATIA. Gehry already had used CATIA for parts of several other buildings, including Fred and Ginger in Prague. But for Bilbao he took full advantage of the computer's modeling possibilities.

How CATIA Works: Digitizing a Physical Model

Here is the CATIA sequence for one of the sections of the Guggenheim Museum in Bilbao

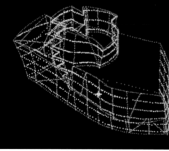

A penlike device traces the shape of the physical model.

Tracing the physical model creates the shape in the computer in the form of a series of rough points.

The rough points are refined, creating an accurate model in the computer.

The computer model is shaded, highlighting the surface shape for initial review.

He says, "Many artists over time have thought about movement, talked about flow. The only thing that holds back or restricts shape is technology and money—because it costs! In our culture technology has evolved so that it's cheaper to build a rectangular building. But if you figure out a way to make technology work for you, you can explore curved shapes and make them possible at competitive costs. You can do this because of the computer."

Gehry doesn't use the computer himself. "I can't stand to look at it for more than four minutes." He designs in drawings and then on physical models of wood, paper, and cloth. So what does CATIA do? The program can turn any wild shape or volume into working drawings. It also talks to other computers—for example, at steel mills and stone quarries— and gives them exact dimensions. With the help of CATIA, Gehry's office

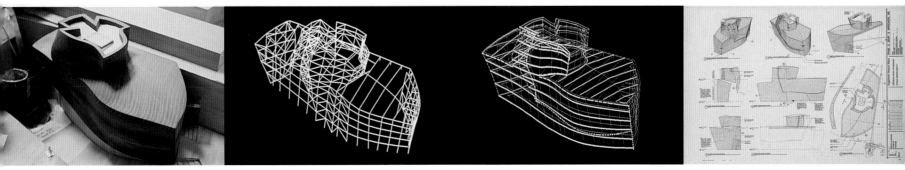

A physical model is created from the computer model for a final review of accuracy.

The computer model is used to create and test the primary building structure in the computer.

The computer model is used to create and test the secondary building structure in the computer.

Drawings to be used during construction are created from the computer model.

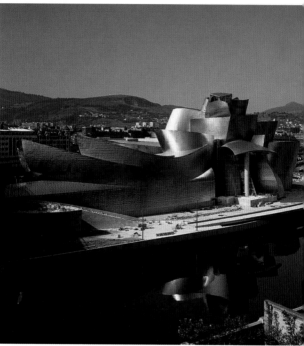

made 565 working drawings and hundreds of models in only two years. Without CATIA it would have taken decades.

Gehry chose titanium, a strong, silvery metal used for missiles, to be the skin of the structure. Even with a budget of one hundred million dollars, the cost was too high. Then someone must have waved a magic wand. The Russians dumped tons of titanium on the market, and the surplus briefly caused the price to drop. It was affordable.

It took four years to build the museum, and when the titanium was installed on the roof, the workers on the top level could see panoramic views of the city and the building blossoming like silver petals beneath them.

For Frank Gehry, who had studied art before he became an architect, Bilbao was his own fantasy come true. "To be at the bend of a working river, connecting the urban fabric of a fairly dense city with a place for modern art, is my idea of heaven." From chain link to titanium: It might seem as if he had come a long way from his bungalow in Santa Monica. But what looks like a giant leap is actually an evolution. You find his fish motif appearing here and there throughout the museum. The metal cladding, seen in his own house and in many other Gehry buildings, reaches its peak in the titanium walls of Bilbao. Jutting skylights, glass partitions,

The outside of the Guggenheim Bilbao is like a piece of sculpture. As you move around, it changes.

(Far left) Down this city boulevard you'll spot a huge, flowering puppy by the American artist Jeff Koons. If you're startled by the bulging metal forms towering behind it, Puppy *lets you know this place is friendly.*

(Top) This grand flagship by Gehry lies moored on the banks of the river surrounded by the city and mountains in the distance. The V-shape of the observation tower anchors the bridge to the building.

(Middle) The titanium panels gleam like fish scales. On this day the building looks like a silver mermaid basking in the sun.

(Bottom) Now you are standing under the La Salve Bridge, which connects one part of the city to the other. People walking or driving over the bridge are enveloped by the ballooning forms.

STONY CREEK LIBRARY
1350 GREENFIELD PIKE
NOBLESVILLE, IN 46060

towers, the cluster of connected spaces: They're all there but grander, more monumental.

He's done it before, Frank admits. "You can't escape your own language."

What about the city of Bilbao? In 1997 its museum opened to rave reviews. AN INSTANT LANDMARK! SPAIN-ISH CONQUEST! BASQUE-ING IN GLORY! read the headlines.

The city hoped it would attract a half million visitors the first year. Instead more

The sights and sounds of the busy city disappear when you go down the wide limestone stairs. Step inside, past the serene limestone lobby in the atrium that soars more than 160 feet high.

Inside and out, this space is not about boxes or straight lines. It speaks of the exhilaration of free-flying forms. Gehry wraps the limestone and titanium materials from the exterior into the interior, contrasting blocks of stone with bending swirls of titanium.

than a million came to marvel at the titanium-clad miracle. It announced the arrival of a new era in architecture, and people wanted to see it for themselves. The streets swarmed with tourists. Bright shops, restaurants, and hotels opened to serve them. The city fathers had asked Frank Gehry for a building that would become a destination, a wonder of the world like the Eiffel Tower or the Pyramids. As it happens in all fairy tales, their wish—with plenty of help from talent and hard work—came true.

Look up; a glass and steel mosaic catches you off guard, tips your balance. The ceiling is like the skeleton of a fish.

Move through the boat gallery. The central gallery is over 430 feet in length, bigger than a football field. The huge steel sculpture by Richard Serra winds down the middle of this lofty room, designed for the largest-scale works of modern artists.

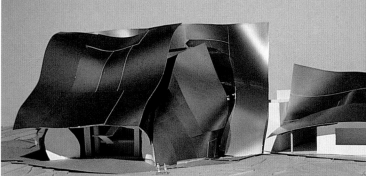

for an encore mr. gehry?

What follows the tremendous success of the Guggenheim in Bilbao? Where does Frank Gehry go from here? Is the pressure on to do something bigger and better? He has won more than one hundred prestigious awards for his architecture, and his desk is piled high with requests from people who want another Bilbao. "The good thing is that my part in Bilbao was over five years ago. So before everyone got excited about it, I'd merrily gone on my way doing what I always did. I'm way beyond Bilbao."

Asked how he reacts to being a celebrity, Gehry says, "The famous thing gets in the way of creativity, especially if a lot of people come in and tell you how great you are and you're scared of this thing you're working on." However, he admits feeling pleased when people on the streets of Bilbao come up and give him a hug.

At seventy Gehry finds his creativity is speeding up. His shapes are becoming looser, flowing even more freely, as if the swelling forms fly, float, and dance from the sheer exuberance of his imagination. "I'm trying to get more liquid, to put feeling and passion and emotion into my buildings through motion."

The Experience Music Project in Seattle rocks and rolls with motion. Actually it's a rock-and-roll museum with the 1962 World's Fair Space Needle for a neighbor and a monorail train running right though the middle. "When I asked the client (Microsoft cofounder and Jimi Hendrix fan Paul Allen) what he was looking for, he said he wanted a building that was 'swoopy.' I said okay. That's what I was interested in. So I made shapes that are swoopy. They come from thinking of

(Opposite, top) Design process model for Millennium Park Music Pavilion, Chicago, Illinois

(Bottom left) Final model for the Experience Music Project, Seattle, Washington

(Bottom right) Model for Bard Center for Performing Arts, Bard College, Annandale-on-Hudson

Jimi Hendrix, broken guitars, Stratoscasters, and shiny surfaces. The red piece in the middle is made out of painted steel. It will fade like an old truck."

But Gehry's projects still make some people nervous. A local opinion poll in Seattle called the Experience Music Project "open-heart surgery gone awry." His Walt Disney Concert Hall in downtown Los Angeles has been delayed for eleven years because of fund-raising problems. Now it's being rushed toward completion. Controversy has never stopped Frank. "I've always thought of myself as radical."

He says, "The difficulty is facing the unknown of the next project. Since I don't repeat myself much, there is a search. You don't know what you're going to do. And if you did, you wouldn't do it. You'd do something else. So searching for the unknown is scary. And the fear fuels creativity, fuels going forward. I've learned to live with that fear and think of it as positive."

Stop by his architectural firm, and you'll see a series of large, open spaces, cluttered with models, computers, and worktables stacked with floor plans and drawings. A team of students and professors from the Massachusetts Institute of Technology (MIT) gather around the model of a new building for the university. Clients from Italy walk in, carrying a coffee cake for the staff. Gehry's assistant runs back and forth ushering people into the studio. With some 250 commissions over a forty-year career, Gehry is busier than ever.

Meanwhile he's started flying lessons, and then there's his monthly ice hockey

Frank Gehry and an associate working on a model

game. The challenges, the process of creating, staying in the game are what excite him. What about the future? Will his museum, which has been called a great masterpiece of our time, be the model for cities of the twenty-first century?

Imagine billowing rooflines gleaming of liquid silver, walls leaning in to embrace you, skylights flooding you with sunlight, the space transforming itself with each step you take.

(Above) Model for Walt Disney Concert Hall, Los Angeles, California

(Inset) Model for concert hall interior

A fantasy? Magic? Gehry's buildings appeal to the magician in all of us.

"I've got other ideas," Frank O. Gehry says, "and now the door is wide open."

glossary

architect—a person whose profession is the design of buildings

architecture—the built environment

asphalt—a black material primarily used for the surface of roofs and roads

beam—a long piece of wood or metal used to support a ceiling, wall, etc.

blueprint—a copy of a plan used as a working drawing

budget—a written statement of the amount of money to be spent on a project

clad—covered in

cladding—the material used to cover a building, such as wood, metal, etc.

client—person who hires a professional, such as an architect, to do a specific job

column—a freestanding vertical

commission—to hire an architect to design a building

construction—the way a building is built

contour line—the outline of a shape

contractor—a person hired to build a building

design—a visual plan

dome—a roof in the form of a half-sphere (circle)

drawing—a sketch or plan in pencil or ink

elevation—the side or end view of a building

exterior—the outside of a building

facade—the front of a building

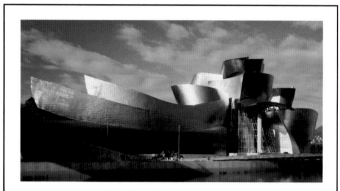

A Leap into Metaphor

Faced with the Guggenheim Bilbao, journalists scale the heights of metaphor (and simile)

- a pile of improbably huge fish
- fractured tinfoil flowers
- a giant whale
- a fantastic dreamship, all sails full, sweeping upstream
- Marilyn Monroe's wind-assisted skirts
- an exploded artichoke heart
- vast hulls of ships that used to loom over shipbuilding towns
- dervishly whirling volumes
- a silver dream machine
- a prehistoric beast advancing with leg and foot toward the water
- an explosion in a sardine factory
- a metallic mountain
- a vast circus tent surrounded by a congeries of caravans
- silver balloons ready to float away
- a monstrous flower
- a fairy-tale castle
- a gigantic game of Chinese boxes within boxes
- a sinuous creature draping its body along a narrow ledge

What does it suggest to you?

forms—shapes

grid—a frame of spaced parallel horizontal and vertical lines

in progress—as used here, a project in some stage of design or building

interior—the inside of a building

joists—parallel wood or steel beams that support floors or ceilings

landscape/landscaping—the planning or arrangement of the land with regard to planting

Le Corbusier—distinguished French modern architect (1887–1966)

master plan—the overall plan for a building or project

models—three-dimensional designs of a building

motif—a theme that is used over and over

organic—referring to a shape that resembles a natural form, such as the human body or a seashell

pitch—the degree of slant of a roof

pitched roof—a slanted roof

plans—a design for the construction of a building

plasterboard—a building material made of plaster of paris and sheets of fiber

program—in architecture, the written purpose of a project, such as the use of the building and the client's needs.

remodel—to remake part or all of an existing building

renovate—to remake, as in remodeling a house

scale—the size, proportion, and relationship of a building to its surroundings

sheathing—a protective covering

shingles—a covering for the roof or sides of a building, often made of wood or asphalt

site—the location of a building

structure—a building made of parts joined together

stucco—an exterior covering for a building, usually a mix of cement and sand

Wright, Frank Lloyd—celebrated American architect to whom Frank Gehry is often compared (1867–1959)

zoning board—a group of community officials who make and enforce rules concerning building and buildings

bibliography

books

- *The Architecture of Frank O. Gehry.* New York: Rizzoli International Publications, 1986.
- Dal Co, Francesco, and Kurt W. Forster. *Frank O. Gehry: The Complete Works.* New York: The Monacelli Press, Inc., 1998.
- Friedman, Mildred, editor, et. al. *Gehry Talks.* New York: Rizzoli International Publications, 1999.
- Steele, James. *Los Angeles Architecture.* London: Phaidon Press Limited, 1993.
- van Bruggen, Coosje. *Frank O. Gehry—Guggenheim Museum Bilbao.* New York: The Solomon R. Guggenheim Foundation & FMGB Guggenheim Bilbao Museoa, 1997.

articles

- Cecelia, F. Marquez, ed. "Frank O. Gehry: 1991–1995." *El Croquis* 74/75 (December 1995).
- "Frank O. Gehry." *El Croquis* 45 (October–November 1990).
- LeCuyer, Annette. "Building Bilbao." *El Croquis* 45.
- Schjeldahl, Peter. "Silver Dream Machine." *Frieze* (November to December 1997).
- Slessor, Catherine. "Atlantic Star." *Architectural Review* (December 1997).
- Sorkin, Michael. "Beyond Bilbao." *Bazaar* (1998).
- Stein, Karen. "Project Diary: Guggenheim Museum Bilbao." *Architectural Record* (October 1997).
- Tomkins, Calvin. "The Maverick." *The New Yorker* (July 1997).

Most quotes taken from the author's interviews with Frank O. Gehry, May 1998 and January 1999. Some remarks taken from a lecture given by Frank O. Gehry at the Architectural League of New York at Town Hall in November 1999.

locations

some cities where you will find work by Frank O. Gehry

Barcelona, Spain: *Monumental Fish Sculpture at Hotel Artes*

Biesfelden, Switzerland: *Vitra International Headquarters*

Bilbao, Spain: *Guggenheim Museum*

Cincinnati, Ohio: *The Vontz Center for Molecular Studies,*
University of Cincinnati

Los Angeles, California: *California Aerospace Museum;*
Loyola Law School; Chiat/Day Headquarters;
The Geffen Contemporary at the Museum of Contemporary Art

Minneapolis, Minnesota: *Frederick R. Weisman Art Museum*

New Haven, Connecticut: *Yale Psychiatric Institute*

Seattle, Washington: *Experience Music Project*

Toledo, Ohio: *Center for the Visual Arts, University of Toledo*

Weil am Rhein, Germany: *Vitra International Design Museum*

California Aerospace Museum

buildings in progress

Annandale-on-Hudson, New York: *Performing Arts Center, Bard College*

Biloxi, Mississippi: *The George Ohr Museum*

Chicago, Illinois: *Millennium Park Music Pavilion*

Cleveland, Ohio: *Weatherhead School of Management, Case Western Reserve University*

Dundee, Scotland: *Maggie's Centre*

El Ciego, Spain: *Marques de Riscal Winery Expansion*

Los Angeles, California: *Walt Disney Concert Hall, Loyola Law School Expansion*

Washington, D.C.: *Corcoran Gallery of Art Expansion*

acknowledgments

Without the cooperation and hard work of many people, a book like this one would not be possible. With deepest thanks to everyone at Frank O. Gehry Associates—especially Berta and Frank Gehry for graciously fitting us into their busy schedules; the resourceful Keith Mendenhall, who promptly answered every question and provided the captions that explain CATIA; Michelle L. Kaufmann, our charming and knowledgeable guide to the Frank Gehry offices; and Chris Herrlinger, Frank's helpful assistant. Thanks to Alejandro Gehry for sharing his thoughts; to Erika Barahona Ede and Marta Iraugui at Guggenheim Bilbao Museoa; to Elaine Blatt, Grant Mudford, and Erica Stoller and her staff at Esto for photography. To Bobbi Katz for her poetry. To computer guru Phil Gordon for his superhuman patience. To Marna Schnabel, Audrey and Arthur Greenberg, and Jackie Greenberg for our "outside in" tour of Frank Gehry sites in Los Angeles, Santa Monica, and Venice. And finally to the ever-terrific people who help us get from manuscript to bound book: our stalwart publisher and editor Neal Porter, inventive designer Dirk Kaufman, production marvel Lou Bilka, effervescent managing editor Laaren Brown, insightful associate editor Beth Sutinis, and discreet assistant Lisa Vargues.

picture credits

Jacket front Jeff Goldberg/Esto; jacket back: Frank Gehry, Erika Barahona Ede © Guggenheim Bilbao; Gehry residence, Jeff Goldberg/Esto; cardboard furniture Frank O. Gehry & Associates; model, Whit Preston, Frank O. Gehry & Associates.

Endpapers. Whit Preston, Frank O. Gehry & Associates; title page, Erika Barahona Ede © FMGB Guggenheim Bilbao.

2-3 © Christian Richters/Esto, 4 (top left) courtesy Frank O. Gehry & Associates, 6 Jeff Goldberg/Esto, 7 Tim Street-Porter/Esto, 8-9 (top) courtesy Frank Gehry , 9 (bottom) AKG London, 10 Erika Barahona Ede © Guggenheim Bilbao, 12 all © Elaine Blatt, 13 Robert Harding Picture Library: Adam Woolfitt/© FLC/ADAGP, Paris and DACS, London 2000, 14 © Grant Mudford, 17 © Tim Street-Porter/Esto, 18 (left and right) © Grant Mudford, 19 © Grant Mudford, 20 (inset and right) courtesy Frank O. Gehry & Associates, 22 courtesy Frank O. Gehry & Associates, 23 (top, second from top, second from bottom, bottom) courtesy Frank O. Gehry & Associates, 24 (large and left inset) © Tim Street-Porter/Esto, 24 (right inset) Robert Harding Picture Library: Roy Rainford, 26 © Grant Mudford, 27(top) © Grant Mudford, 28 (top) © Grant Mudford, 29 © Tim Griffith/Esto, 30 Everett/Corbis, 31 © Tim Griffith/Esto, 32-33 Erika Barahona Ede © Guggenheim Bilbao, 32 (inset) Erika Barahona Ede © Guggenheim Bilbao, 34 David Heald © The Solomon R. Guggenheim Foundation, New York, 34–35 CATIA process courtesy Frank O. Gehry & Associates, 35 (upper) Erika Barahona Ede © FMGB Guggenheim Bilbao, 36 (left) Erika Barahona Ede © FMGB Guggenheim Bilbao, 36 (top and bottom) Erika Barahona Ede © Guggenheim Bilbao, (middle) Jeff Goldberg/Esto, 38 (left) Jeff Goldberg/Esto, (middle) Erika Barahona Ede © Guggenheim Bilbao, 39 (left) Christian Richters/Esto, (right) Erika Barahona Ede © Guggenheim Bilbao, 40 (top) Whit Preston/Frank O. Gehry & Associates, (bottom left & right) courtesy Frank O. Gehry & Associates, 42 (bottom) courtesy Frank O. Gehry & Associates, 43 (top and inset) courtesy Frank O. Gehry & Associates, 44 Jeff Goldberg/Esto, 47 © Timothy Hursley

Sketches, drawings: pages 4, 5, 23, 27, 33, 42 Frank Gehry, © Frank O. Gehry.

8 Standing Glass Fish, Frank Gehry, 1986, wood, glass, steel, silicone, Plexiglas, rubber, size 264 x 168 x 102 inches, Walker Art Center, Gift of Anne Pierce Rogers in honor of her grandchildren, Anne and Will Rogers, 1986.

28 Design for a Theater Library for Venice in the Form of Binoculars and Coltello Ship in Three Stages 1984, Claes Oldenburg and Coosje van Bruggen, Pencil, colored pencil, chalk, watercolor, 30 x 40 inches (76 x 101.6 cm.)